Du...

Home to the Cham...
Riverside hosted its first Test match in 2003.

The Riverside Ground
Main tel 0191 387 1717
Website www.durhamccc.co.uk
Ends Finchale End, Lumley End
Capacity 7,000 (16,000 with temporary seating)
First County Match Durham v Warwickshire (18 May 1995)
First Test Match England v Zimbabwe (5 June 2003)
First ODI Pakistan v Scotland (20 May 1999)
Record crowd 16,000 England v Australia ODI (23 June 2005)
Formed in 1882 (admitted to the Championship in 1992)
County Champions 2008, 2009
Gillette/NatWest/C&G/FP 2007
Benson & Hedges Best – Quarter-finals 1998, 2000, 2001
Sunday League Best – 6th (Div One) 2009
Twenty20 Best – Semi-finals 2008
Nickname of one-day team Dynamos
Leading run-scorer Jon Lewis (1997-2006) 7,854 (av 31.41)
Leading wicket-taker Simon Brown (1992-2002) 518 (av 28.30)
Most wicket-keeping dismissals Phil Mustard (2002-) 359 (346 ct, 13 st)
Most capped England player Steve Harmison (1996-) 62 Tests

Durham won its first match against Northumberland in June 1882, played at Ashbrooke Cricket Ground, Sunderland. It soon established itself as a formidable force in Minor Counties cricket where it first played in 1899, winning five championships by 1930. It then endured a 46-year barren spell (including the ignominy of finishing bottom in 1953), before regaining its dominant status from 1976 onwards. The club achieved the record for the longest unbeaten spell in Minor Counties cricket, spanning 65 matches between 1976 and 1982 (the Championship was won in three of those seasons) and in 1984 won the Minor Counties title for the ninth time.

In 1973 Durham had become the first Minor Counties side to defeat a first-class county when they toppled Yorkshire in the Gillette Cup. In 1985 they beat Derbyshire in the NatWest Trophy, to become the first Minor County to defeat a first-class team twice.

In 1989 the board of Durham Cricket Club applied for first-class status, which was granted in December 1991. Durham played in the County Championship for the first time in 1992 season. Their very first match was against Leicestershire at the Racecourse Ground in Durham. Until the construction of the new ground at the Riverside, Durham played at a variety of grounds in the county.

Durham took a while to adjust to the higher standards of first-class cricket, finishing in the bottom three of the Championship in each of their first six seasons. However, with the help of experienced professionals the county made progress. This improvement culminated in 2007 when the club won its first major title, the one-day Friends Provident Trophy, followed by Championships in both 2008 and 2009.

In 1993, a year after being granted first-class status, Durham received permission to build its own ground at the Riverside. Opened in 1995, Durham played their first match there against Warwickshire. In October 1996, the Queen officially opened the Don Robson Pavilion. There are six permanent stands on the western and southern ends, while the northern and eastern sides have tiered tip-up seats.

In 1999 the Riverside hosted two World Cup matches. The following year an England one-day international was held against the West Indies. England's Test Match against Zimbabwe in June 2003 marked the historic occasion of the first Test at the Riverside.

Essex were formed in 1876 but had to wait for more than a century before enjoying the most successful spell in their history. They won their first County Championship in 1979 and five more between then and 1992, together with an array of one-day titles. Led by inspirational captains Keith Fletcher and Graham Gooch, Essex enjoyed a golden age in their cricketing history.

Essex County Cricket Club was established on 14 January 1876, and played its opening first-class match against Leicestershire at Leyton in May 1894. In 1895 it was admitted to the Championship and finished ninth under the leadership of HG Owen; the team soon made huge strides vying for the title for much of the 1897 season and eventually finished third.

The county began to produce some talented players who made their mark. PA Perrin scored nearly 30,000 runs in first-class cricket, including 66 centuries, but was never picked for England. Under the captaincy of JWHT Douglas, who led the team from 1911 to 1928, performances steadily improved. The leg-spin bowler Peter Smith made his debut in 1929 and was a key part of the side in the 1930s, as was batsman Jack O'Connor, who scored over 1,000 runs in each of 15 consecutive seasons in the run-up to the Second World War.

Following the sale of their main ground at Leyton in 1933, Essex moved between nine different grounds over successive decades, until Chelmsford became their permanent headquarters in 1967. The post-War era produced such distinguished cricketers as Doug Insole, who captained the team from 1950 and was its most reliable batsman, and all-rounder Trevor Bailey,

a key player for England in the 1950s (as well as Insole's successor as Essex captain). Yet the county found consistency elusive, and it suffered the ignominy of picking up the Championship wooden spoon in 1950.

But the 1970s, and in particular Fletcher assuming the captaincy in 1974, marked the beginning of the renaissance. For the next 20 years, the county's devoted following were treated to many titles. The disappointment of a second place finish in 1978, largely due to bad luck with the weather, was followed by the club's first Championship triumph in 1979. This triumph was resounding, as 13 matches were won in the season, and the county also picked up the Benson and Hedges Cup. Further trophies were won during the 1980s and 1990s in both the long and the short version of the game, and a number of Essex heroes went on to play for England, including captains Graham Gooch and Nasser Hussain.

Essex first staged a Championship match at Chelmsford in 1926, against Somerset. However, it was not until 1967 that Chelmsford became the permanent home of Essex cricket. The pavilion was completed in 1970 and other stands have been added since. In 2002 floodlights were installed. At the ground, Essex have enjoyed the most successful spell in their history, becoming a force to be reckoned with in the English county game. During this period, Graham Gooch scored 8,710 runs at an average of 54.77 at Chelmsford, including his highest score for the county, 275 made against Kent in 1988. The county currently have plans to redevelop the Chelmsford ground. This will increase the capacity to 8,000.

THE FORD COUNTY GROUND, CHELMSFORD

Main tel 01245 252420
Website www.essexcricket.org.uk
Capacity 8,000

First County Match Essex v Oxford University (20 June 1925)
First ODI Australia v India (20 June 1983)
Record crowd 7,300 – Twenty20, Essex v Kent (20 June 2003)
Formed in 1876 (admitted to the Championship in 1895)
County Champions 1979, 1983, 1984, 1986, 1991, 1992

Pavilion

River Can

Hayes Close End

River End

Score board

A1060

Gillette/NatWest/C&G/FP 1985, 1997, 2008
Benson & Hedges 1979, 1998
Sunday League 1981, 1984, 1985, 2005, 2006
Twenty20 Best – Semi-finals 2006, 2007
Nickname of one-day team Eagles
Leading run-scorer Graham Gooch (1973-97) 30,701 (av 51.77)
Leading wicket-taker Peter Smith (1929-51) 1,610 (av 26.68)
Most wicket-keeping dismissals Brian Taylor (1949-73) 1,231 (1,040 ct, 191 st)
Most capped England player Graham Gooch (1973-97) – 118 Tests

ESSEX

One of the strongest County sides, since the late seventies Essex has had a tremendous run of success — to the delight of their enthusiatic local supporters.

GLAMORGAN

Home to Glamorgan Cricket Club since 1967, the SWALEC Stadium hosted its first Test match in the summer of 2009.

Glamorgan CCC was founded in 1888. It competed in the Minor County Championship until, in 1921, it successfully applied to join the County Championship – the last county to do so until Durham 70 years later. It started encouragingly, winning its first match, against Sussex, but thereafter its results were so poor that *Wisden* expressed the view that its entry into first-class cricket had not been justified by results. Of its three professional players, two were 47 years old! The rest of the team was made up of a number of mediocre amateurs.

In 1930 Maurice Turnbull, who the previous winter had become the first Glamorgan player to be capped by England, became Glamorgan captain. He also became the club secretary. Turnbull held both positions throughout the 1930s, and as well as improving the club's financial position, he helped to set up a settled team with a core of useful professional players.

In 1948, under the captaincy of all-rounder Wilfred Wooller, Glamorgan won the Championship. In the next few years the club were unable to repeat that success, although their team included Allan Watkins, Jim McConnon, Gilbert Parkhouse and Don Shepherd.

After finishing second in 1963, and third in both 1965 and 1968, in 1969 Glamorgan won the Championship again, under the captaincy of Tony Lewis. The first county since Lancashire in 1930 to go through the season undefeated, the team featured the batting of Lewis, Alan Jones and the Pakistani Majid Khan, the all-round skills of Peter Walker, and the bowling of Shepherd, Tony Cordle and Malcolm Nash. The 1970s and 1980s were lean years for Glamorgan cricket, with one of the few highlights occurring in 1977 when Alan Jones led them to the final of the Gillette Cup. The county had eight captains in less than a decade.

A revival occurred in the 1990s. Viv Richards helped Glamorgan win the Sunday League in 1993 and another destructive batsman, Matthew Maynard, led Glamorgan to their third Championship in 1997. That side, coached by Duncan Fletcher, also featured opening batsman Steve James, who in 2000 went on to make the first triple century for Glamorgan, and Pakistani Waqar Younis. Sunday League triumphs followed in 2002 and 2004.

Glamorgan first played at Sophia Gardens in 1967, after the cricket ground at Cardiff Arms Park had been subsumed within a new national rugby stadium. The ground is to the north of the ornamental gardens named after Sophia, the wife of the second Marquess of Bute, who laid out recreational grounds for the use of the residents of Cardiff.

For the first time in its history Glamorgan had its own permanent ground when, in 1995, the club acquired a 125-year lease of Sophia Gardens. It has since developed the ground as its headquarters, with a National Cricket Centre, which was opened in 1999. After 18 months' substantial refurbishment and rebuilding work, which transformed the ground's capacity from 6,500 to 16,000, a new stadium was opened in May 2008. Renamed the SWALEC Stadium under a 10-year, £1.5m sponsorship deal with an energy supplier, the second phase of the building works was completed in time for the first Test Match, the Ashes opener, in July 2009.

THE SWALEC STADIUM, CARDIFF

Main tel 0871 282 3401
Website www.glamorgancricket.com
Capacity 16,000
First County Match Glamorgan v Indians (24 May 1967)
First Test Match England v Australia (8 July 2009)
First ODI Australia v New Zealand (20 May 1999)
Record crowd 16,000 England v Australia (both 8 and 9 July 2009)
Formed in 1888 (admitted to the Championship in 1921)
County Champions 1948, 1969, 1997
Gillette/NatWest/C&G/FP Best – Runners-up 1977

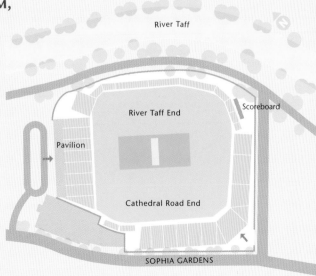

River Taff

River Taff End

Scoreboard

Pavilion

Cathedral Road End

SOPHIA GARDENS

Benson & Hedges Best – Runners-up 2000
Sunday League 1993, 2002, 2004
Twenty20 Best – Semi-finals 2004
Nickname of one-day team Dragons
Leading run-scorer Alan Jones (1957-83) 34,056 (av 33.03)
Leading wicket-taker Don Shepherd (1950-72) 2,174 (av 20.95)
Most wicket-keeping dismissals Eifion Jones (1961-83) 933 (840 ct, 93 st)
Most capped England player Robert Croft (1989-) – 21 Tests

Whilst the first recorded cricket match in Gloucestershire took place as early as 1729, the present club was founded in 1870 or 1871. WG Grace was captain for three decades and during the 1870s the nucleus of the team was provided by the three Grace brothers, WG, EM and GF, all three of whom played in the first Test Match in England in 1880.

Between 1873 and 1881 Gloucestershire won the unofficial championship four times (once shared) and were runners-up three times. Since the reorganisation of the County Championship in 1890, Gloucestershire have never won the title, although they have endured the frustration of finishing second on six occasions. This is surprising in view of the numerous exceptional match-winning players in their teams. Two notable all-rounders at the turn of the 20th century were Charles Townsend, who in 1899 scored 2,440 runs and the legendary big-hitter Gilbert Jessop. Captain between 1900 and 1912, Jessop led from the front with his unorthodox but mightily effective batting, fast bowling and brilliant cover-point fielding.

Results, however, were moderate, and remained so until Beverley Lyon became captain in 1929. Although short of pace bowling, Lyon's team included three all-time greats: the incomparable Walter Hammond, the finest English batsman of his generation and a heavy run-scorer for his county – he headed the English first-class averages for eight years in a row; and the spinners Charlie Parker and Tom Goddard, who took a combined aggregate of more than 6,000 first-class wickets. In both 1930 and 1931 Lyon's inventive captaincy led Gloucestershire to second place in the Championship.

Goddard's bowling – at the age of 46 he took a county record 222 wickets – helped the club to challenge for the Championship in 1947, but Compton and Edrich's Middlesex were even mightier, winning a crucial match between the two sides by 68 runs despite Goddard taking 15 wickets. In 1959 Tom Graveney led a team notable for its incisive bowling – especially the off-spin of David Brown and John Mortimore – to second place once again.

A decade of decline followed Graveney's removal as captain and his resulting decision to move to Worcestershire, but all-rounder Tony Brown proved to be a doughty captain, leading Gloucestershire to yet another second place in the Championship and, in 1973, to their first trophy, the Gillette Cup. The explosive all-round skills of Mike Procter provided the most telling contribution to the county's successes in that period, so much so that the county was nicknamed "Proctershire". Procter went on to lead the side to the B&H Cup in 1977, helped by the silky batting of the prolific Zaheer Abbas.

At the turn of the 21st century, under the captaincy of Mark Alleyne and the coaching of New Zealander John Bracewell, Gloucestershire enjoyed considerable one-day success, winning six trophies in five years. Key to those triumphs were the fast bowling of Mike Smith and Courtney Walsh and the wicket-keeping of the idiosyncratic "Jack" Russell.

The County Ground has been Gloucestershire's headquarters for 120 years. Twice, in 1919 and 1976, the club sold the ground, only to buy it back, most recently in 2004. Situated in the northern outskirts of Bristol, it has the second largest playing area in English cricket – and is redolent with cricketing history.

THE COUNTY GROUND, BRISTOL

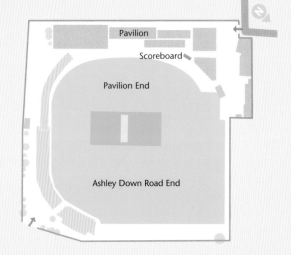

Main tel 0117 910 8000
Website www.gloscricket.co.uk
Capacity 3,600 (15,000 with temporary seating for ODIs)

First County Match Gloucestershire v Lancashire (1 July 1889)
First ODI New Zealand v Sri Lanka (13 June 1983)
Record crowd 16,000 ODI England v India (24 August 2007)
Formed in 1871
County Champions Best – Runners-up in 1930, 1931, 1947, 1959, 1969, 1986
Gillette/NatWest/C&G/FP 1973, 1999, 2000, 2003, 2004
Benson & Hedges 1977, 1999, 2000

Map labels: Pavilion; Scoreboard; Pavilion End; Ashley Down Road End

Sunday League Best – Runners-up 1988
Twenty20 Best – Runners-up 2007
Nickname of one-day team Gladiators
Leading run-scorer Walter Hammond (1920-51) 33,664 (av 57.05)
Leading wicket-taker Charlie Parker (1903-35) 3,170 (av 19.43)
Most wicket-keeping dismissals "Jack" Russell (1981-2004) 1,054 (950 ct, 104 st)
Most capped England player Walter Hammond (1920-51) – 85 Tests

GLOUCESTERSHIRE

The County Ground at Nevil Road, Bristol was purchased and established by WG Grace, Gloucestershire's first captain.

HAMPSHIRE

Opened in 2001, the dramatic Rose Bowl in Southampton is the most recently established first-class County ground.

THE ROSE BOWL, SOUTHAMPTON

Main tel 023 8047 2002
Website www.rosebowlplc.com/home/
hampshire-cricket
Capacity 9,800 (20,000 with temporary
seating)

First County Match Hampshire v
Worcestershire (9 May 2001)
First ODI South Africa v Zimbabwe
(10 July 2003)
First Test Match Due June 2011
Record crowd 20,000 Twenty20 Final
Kent v Middlesex (26 July 2008)
Formed in 1863 (admitted to the
Championship in 1895)
County Champions 1961, 1973
Gillette/NatWest/C&G/FP 1991, 2005, 2009
Benson & Hedges 1988, 1992

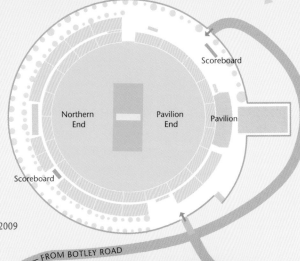

Scoreboard

Northern
End

Pavilion
End

Pavilion

Scoreboard

FROM BOTLEY ROAD

Sunday League 1975, 1978,
1986
Twenty20 Best – Quarter-
finals 2004
Nickname of one-day team
Hawks
Leading run-scorer Phil Mead
(1905-36) 48,892 (av 48.84)
Leading wicket-taker Derek
Shackleton (1948-69) 2,669
(av 18.23)
**Most wicket-keeping
dismissals** Bobby Parks
(1980-92) 700 (630 ct, 70 st)
Most capped England player
Robin Smith (1982-2003) –
62 Tests

Hampshire have enjoyed a high-profile in recent years, especially since their move to the Rose Bowl in 2001. The county enjoyed their most successful period in the 1960s and 1970s, winning their first two County Championship titles and a number of one-day titles.

Whilst the club was established in 1863, the origins of cricket in the county run a lot deeper. The cricket played there revolved around the Hambledon Cricket Club, which had become a leading side by the 1760s and was integral to the establishment of the county side. Hampshire made their first-class debut in 1864. Although they lost their unofficial first-class status in 1886 after a string of poor results, they returned to the elite of English cricket through their admission to the fledgling Championship in 1895. They struggled at first – in the seasons between 1900 and 1906, for instance, they were usually at the bottom of the Championship.

The dismal run of form was stemmed by an eighth place finish in 1906 under the leadership of EM Sprot. The arrival of prolific batsman Phil Mead and the blossoming of a number of players took the county to a record fifth position in 1914. No one has scored more runs for any county than the 48,892 runs Mead accumulated for Hampshire. His total of 55,061 first-class runs, including 153 hundreds, makes him the fourth highest run-scorer in all first-class cricket. Also in the same team as Mead were Jack Newman and Alec Kennedy, who were consistent all-round cricketers for Hampshire until the 1930s. Another influential figure was Lionel Tennyson (later Lord Tennyson) who arrived in 1913 and was captain from 1919 to 1933. The county's performances picked up; between 1920 and 1930 its average position was 11th, although for most of the 1930s it gravitated towards the lower reaches of the table.

After the War, Desmond Eagar assumed the captaincy and soon the Hampshire attack was being led by Derek Shackleton and HD Cannings. The attacking left-handed batsman, Colin Ingleby-Mackenzie, came into the side in 1951 and seven years later succeeded Eagar as captain. Under his leadership, Hampshire won their first Championship in 1961, winning 19 out of 32 matches; ten of their victories came from declarations, which was testament to Ingleby-Mackenzie's flair and tactical nous. Substantial contributions were made by Jimmy Gray, Henry Horton and Roy Marshall, all of whom exceeded 2,000 runs, and the indefatigable Shackleton, who took 153 wickets.

Hampshire's second Championship came in 1973, under the leadership of Richard Gilliat, during a successful period for the club which coincided with the recruitment of outstanding overseas players including opening batsmen Gordon Greenidge and Barry Richards, and paceman Andy Roberts; it also won two one-day league titles in the 1970s. More recently it has continued the tradition of one-day success, with five trophies won in this format between 1986 and 2005. Another West Indian, Malcolm Marshall, made a massive contribution to the earlier of these one-day titles and was a Hampshire stalwart (in 210 first-class matches for Hampshire he took 826 wickets at an average of 18.64 and also scored 5,847 runs). Other key players at the time included Mark Nicholas, who became captain in 1985, and the England batsman Robin Smith.

The county has had several high-profile players in recent times, notably the flamboyant Australian spin bowler Shane Warne (including a spell as captain when he nurtured some of the younger players) and the swashbuckling England batsman Kevin Pietersen. It has also moved to a brand new ground, the Rose Bowl, which has already played host to one-day internationals.

Built with the intention of bringing Test cricket to the south coast, Hampshire's Rose Bowl hosted its first match in 2001, when the visitors were Essex in the Benson & Hedges zonal round. The inaugural first-class match took place soon after, with the visitors being Worcestershire. Perhaps the highlight of the first season at the Rose Bowl for home fans was when the touring Australians were bowled out for 97.

Construction of the ground began in 1997, soon after Hampshire had sold its Northlands Road stadium and secured £7.2m of Heritage Lottery funding. It is a circular amphitheatre, boasting a three-floor pavilion. Its international debut came when it hosted a match between South Africa and Zimbabwe in 2003. It was the venue for England's first Twenty20 International, played against Australia in 2005, and is due to host its first Test Match in 2011. It has been given strong financial support by businessman Rod Bransgrove, who became Hampshire chairman in 2000.

Plans were recently announced to further develop the ground increasing its capacity from 20,000 to 25,000 by adding a pair of matching stands on either side of the pavilion and a new stand at the Northern End. As a result of this proposal, the number of permanent seats will increase by 15,000, of which 6,000 will be under cover. The new development also includes a 175-bedroom hotel. Work on the £48m redevelopment project began in November 2009. The Rose Bowl is also a venue for concerts.

Kent Cricket Club was formed in Canterbury in 1842 and became the champion county in 1843, 1847 and 1849, although these were unofficial titles. In 1859, following amalgamation with the Canterbury club, Kent CCC was formed. The team competed in the County Championship when the competition was formalised in 1890.

Lord Harris, who made his Kent debut in 1870, was appointed captain in 1875, and maintained an association with the county for more than 60 years. Kent have enjoyed two particularly successful eras, accumulating seven Championships in the process. During the first of these, between 1906 and 1913, they won four Championships, under the captaincy of Cloudesley Marsham and then Ted Dillon.

After the First World War, Kent struggled to maintain their success. While they came close to winning the Championship in 1919, later years were characterised by sporadic brilliance but inconsistency. There were some high-calibre players, such as wicket-keepers Les Ames and Godfrey Evans and the prodigiously talented Colin Cowdrey. Cowdrey first played for Kent in 1950, and was appointed captain in 1956, a position he held until 1971.

Kent did not become a consistently successful force in the game again until the 1970s, although in both 1967 and 1968 they finished runners-up in the Championship to Yorkshire. Three further Championships were won in 1970, 1977 and 1978, alongside a string of one-day trophies. These included three Sunday League victories (in 1972, 1973 and 1976) and three B&H Cup victories (in 1973, 1976 and 1978). Their success was built on the batting of Cowdrey, Asif Iqbal, Brian Luckhurst and Mike Denness (who was captain between 1972 and 1976) and the wicket-keeping of Alan Knott, as well as the spin-bowling of Derek Underwood. The team have continued to pick up titles, capturing the Sunday League title in 1995 and 2001, and the Twenty20 Trophy in 2007.

Canterbury is one of the most idyllic settings for cricket in England. The St Lawrence Ground, which took its name from a nearby hospital, was opened in 1847. The Canterbury Cricket Week, which takes place in early August, dates from that time. In 1876 the ground was the scene for WG Grace's highest first-class innings, 344 for the MCC against Kent.

The ground was acquired by Kent in 1896 for £4,500. At the time the only structure on the site was a thatched shed. A pavilion was opened in 1900, which was eventually rebuilt and extended in 1970 when it became the Stuart Chiesman Pavilion. The ground has a number of stands named after Kent heroes, including the Leslie Ames Stand (now consisting of hospitality boxes), the Frank Woolley Stand and the Colin Cowdrey Stand, completed in 1986 at a cost of £600,000.

The most famous landmark associated with the ground is the tree located on the outfield. Any shot which hit the tree was deemed a four. Although the original lime tree (thought to be 180 years old) blew down in a storm in 2005, another tree was planted in March 2005. The historic tree was cleared by the West Indian batsman Carl Hooper in his very first match for Kent (against Durham in 1994), the third time this is known to have happened. This picturesque ground has hosted a number of one-day internationals, including England's victory over Kenya in the 1999 World Cup.

THE ST LAWRENCE GROUND, CANTERBURY

Main tel 01227 456886
Website www.kentccc.co.uk
Capacity 10,000

First County Match Kent v England (2 August 1847)
First ODI England v Kenya (18 May 1999)
Record crowd 23,000 Kent v The Australians (23 August 1948)
Formed in 1859
County Champions 1906, 1909, 1910, 1913, 1970, 1977 (shared), 1978
Gillette/NatWest/C&G/FP 1967, 1974
Benson & Hedges 1973, 1976, 1978
Sunday League 1972, 1973, 1976, 1995, 2001
Twenty20 2007

NACKINGTON ROAD
Scoreboard
Nackington Road End
OLD DOVER ROAD
Pavilion End
Scoreboard

Nickname of one-day team Spitfires
Leading run-scorer Frank Woolley (1906-38) 47,868 (av 41.77)
Leading wicket-taker "Tich" Freeman (1914-36) 3,340 (av 17.64)
Most wicket-keeping dismissals Frank Huish (1895-1914) 1,253 (901 ct, 352 st)
Most capped England player Colin Cowdrey (1950-76) – 114 Tests

KENT

County cricket has been played at the beautiful St Lawrence Ground in Canterbury since 1847 – long before the establishment of the Championship.

LANCASHIRE

Old Trafford first hosted a Test match as early as 1884 and has been the scene of many Test and County rivalries in the intervening years.

OLD TRAFFORD

Main tel 0161 282 4000
Website www.lccc.co.uk
Capacity 17,000
(with temporary seating 21,500)

First County Match
Lancashire
v Middlesex (20 July 1865)
First Test Match England
v Australia (10 July 1884)
First ODI England v
Australia (24 August 1972)
Record crowd 46,000,
Lancashire v Yorkshire
(31 July 1926)

TALBOT ROAD

BRIAN STATHAM WAY

Pavilion

Scoreboard

Stretford End

Brian
Statham
End

Scoreboard

Formed in 1864
County Champions 1897, 1904, 1926, 1927, 1928, 1930, 1934, 1950 (shared)
Gillette/NatWest/C&G/FP 1970, 1971, 1972, 1975, 1990, 1996, 1998
Benson & Hedges 1984, 1990, 1995, 1996
Sunday League 1969, 1970, 1989, 1998
Twenty20 Best – Runners-up 2005
Nickname of one-day team Lightning
Leading run-scorer Ernest Tyldesley (1909-36) 34,222 (av 45.20)
Leading wicket-taker Brian Statham (1950-68) 1,816 (av 15.12)
Most wicket-keeping dismissals George Duckworth (1923-38) 925 (635 ct, 290 st)
Most capped England player Mike Atherton (1987-2001) – 115 Tests

Above: Old Trafford. The site has been used for cricket since the mid 19th century; in 1884 it became the second ground, after The Oval, to stage Test cricket. During the First World War Old Trafford was used as a hospital and over 1,800 patients were treated there. In the Second World War it was used by the army as a transit camp and suffered severe air-raid damage.

Lancashire have a proud history stretching back to 1864, and have produced a series of idiosyncratic characters, many of them brought to life by Sir Neville Cardus in the *Manchester Guardian*.

The year 1867 saw the first Roses Match against Yorkshire, and the debut of AN "Monkey" Hornby, who made a major contribution to Lancashire's development over the next 50 years, both as a hard-driving batsman, as captain (1880-93 and again, in his early 50s, in 1897 and 1898), and as President between 1894 and 1916. He formed a famous opening partnership with RG Barlow, who carried his bat through an innings 12 times.

Under Hornby, Lancashire won the Championship in 1897, notable contributions being made by slow left-armer Johnny Briggs, fast bowler Arthur Mold and the majestic batsman Archie MacLaren, who two years earlier, against Somerset at Taunton, scored 424 – still the highest score by an Englishman in first-class cricket. MacLaren went on to lead Lancashire to Championship triumph in 1904 without losing a match.

Lancashire enjoyed a golden era between the Wars, picking up five Championships in nine seasons, three of them, between 1926 and 1928, under the leadership of Major Green in the only years he captained the county. Ted McDonald, the Australian paceman with a gliding action, took 484 Championship wickets in those three years, and was supported by the wide-girthed leg-spinner Richard Tyldesley with 303 wickets. A formidable batting line-up was headed by Charles Hallows – who in 1928 scored 1,000 runs in May alone and a county record 11 hundreds – and Ernest Tyldesley, who in 1926 enjoyed a remarkable sequence of a record ten 50s (seven of them centuries) in successive innings. Key contributions to the Championship wins in 1930 and 1934 were made by determined left-hander Eddie Paynter and the all-rounder Len Hopwood.

After the Second World War, Lancashire's batting was dominated by its opening pair, Winston Place and Cyril Washbrook, both of whom passed 2,500 runs in 1947. A shared Championship in 1950 owed much to the spin bowling of Roy Tattersall, who took 153 wickets, and Malcolm Hilton, and the emergence of Lancashire's leading wicket-taker, the accurate pace bowler Brian Statham.

Washbrook proved to be a safe but uninspired first professional captain of the county in the mid-1950s. The young Bob Barber almost led Lancashire to the Championship in 1960, a year in which Statham, fellow-paceman Ken Higgs and leg-spinner Tommy Greenhough

all exceeded 100 wickets, but the next few years were less harmonious for the county.

A happier era dawned in 1968 with the appointment of Jack Bond as captain. In his five years at the helm, the county won the Gillette Cup three times and the Sunday League twice and challenged for the Championship. Overseas signings Clive Lloyd and Farokh Engineer particularly galvanised the team in the one-day game, with fast-scoring batting from David Lloyd, Barry Wood, Harry Pilling and Frank Hayes and a bowling attack featuring pacemen Peter Lever and Peter Lee and the canny flat off-spin of Jack Simmons.

After a blip in the early 1980s, Lancashire recovered in 1987 to finish runners-up in the Championship, with important batting contributions from Graeme Fowler, Neil Fairbrother and a youngster from Cambridge University, Mike Atherton. Further one-day trophies followed: in both 1990 and 1996 Lancashire carried off the double of winning the Lord's finals of both of the two knock-out competitions. The Pakistani fast bowler Wasim Akram was a formidable weapon.

The Championship crown has, however, proved frustratingly elusive: Lancashire were second again in 1998, 1999, 2000 and 2003, immediately bounced back from relegation in 2004 to promotion as Division Two champions the following year and were Championship runners-up again in 2006.

Old Trafford has been the home of Manchester Cricket Club since 1856 and of Lancashire CCC since its foundation eight years later. Originally leased, the ground was bought from the de Trafford family (from whom the ground's name derives) in 1898 for £24,082. In 1884 Old Trafford became the second ground in England, after The Oval, to host a Test Match. On the second day of the match 12,000 cricket fans came to see England play Australia. However, Old Trafford has the reputation of being the wettest of Test grounds.

Since the 1880s, Old Trafford has hosted many famous Tests. They include the Ashes Tests of 1896, when Ranjitsinhji hit a glorious 154 not out on his Test debut; 1902, when Victor Trumper scored a century before lunch on the first day of the Test and Australia went on to win a thriller by three runs; 1956, when Jim Laker performed his famous (and still unique) feat of taking 19 Australian wickets; and 1981, featuring Ian Botham's dashing century.

Originally amateurs and professionals would walk onto the field at Old Trafford through different gates. In 1902 this tradition was abolished, even if they still maintained separate changing rooms.

Grace Ground was opened in 1878 and Leicestershire CCC was formed the following year. The club performed well in the second-class championship – in 1888 it won the championship and defeated the touring Australians – and in 1895 joined the County Championship.

Under the captaincy of the big-hitting CE de Trafford, Leicestershire finished fifth in 1905, a result that was not improved upon for almost 50 years.

After the Second World War the prolific opening bat Les Berry was captain for three years. However, the county's revival came with the recruitment of Charles Palmer, who was an inspiring captain between 1950 and 1957 and led Leicestershire to third place in 1953.

Leicestershire's policy of recruiting experienced players from other counties to captain the side bore fruit first with the former Yorkshire batsman Willie Watson (captain 1958-1961), then with Tony Lock, who led the county to joint second place in 1967 and, most of all, with Ray Illingworth (captain 1969-1978).

In partnership with secretary manager Mike Turner, Illingworth led Leicestershire to its first trophy – the B&H Cup – in 1972, the Sunday League followed in 1974 (and again in 1977) and in 1975 came the notable double of the B&H Cup and the county's first ever Championship. Substantial contributions were made by batsmen Brian Davison, Chris Balderstone, Barry Dudleston and John Steele: in 1979 the latter two shared an opening stand of 390, the club's highest partnership ever in county cricket.

In 1985 the elegant left-hander David Gower led Leicestershire to a further B&H Cup, assisted by the gritty all-rounder Peter Willey and the fast bowling of Jonathan Agnew. After being runners-up in 1994, further County Championship titles followed in 1996 and 1998. These were team efforts, under captain James Whitaker and coach Jack Birkenshaw, who had previously made notable all-round contributions to Illingworth's triumphs in the 1970s. However, success could not be sustained. Despite the determined captaincy of Paul Nixon and the batting of Hylton Ackerman – who in 2006 scored the second triple century ever for the club – results have not improved. Two Twenty20 Cup trophies have been insufficient consolation.

The history of Grace Road dates from 1877 when Leicestershire County Cricket Ground Co Ltd purchased 16 acres of land from the Duke of Rutland and laid out the ground. The following year, an estimated 30,000 spectators watched the Australians play Leicestershire. Subsequently, crowds at Grace Road tended to be small, as it was far from Leicester town centre and had poor transport links – only horse trams came to Grace Road. As a result, the county moved to the more central Aylestone Road ground in 1901 and sold Grace Road.

When, in 1945, the club's lease on Aylestone Road (which had been damaged during the war) was not renewed, the county returned again to Grace Road. The ground was gradually redeveloped after being bought by the club in 1966, with a new pavilion, indoor school, media centre and museum. This redevelopment led to Grace Road hosting one-day internationals for the first time. What was formerly known as the Hawkesbury Road End is now the Bennett End, in recognition of the benefactor Trevor Bennett MBE.

GRACE ROAD, LEICESTER

Main tel 0871 282 1879
Website www.leicestershireccc.co.uk
Capacity 6,000

First County Match Leicestershire v Yorkshire (17 May 1894)
First ODI India v Zimbabwe (11 June 1983)
Record crowd 6,000 Twenty20 Quarter-final Leicestershire v Kent (24 July 2006)

Formed in 1879 (admitted to the Championship in 1895)
County Champions 1975, 1996, 1998
Gillette/NatWest/C&G/FP Best – Runners-up 1992, 2001
Benson & Hedges 1972, 1975, 1985
Sunday League 1974, 1977

MILLIGAN ROAD

Scoreboard

Pavilion

Pavilion End

Bennett End

Scoreboard

Twenty20 2004, 2006
Nickname of one-day team Foxes

Leading run-scorer Les Berry (1924-51) 30,143 (av 30.32)
Leading wicket-taker Ewart Astill (1906-39) 2,131 (av 23.18)
Most wicket-keeping dismissals Roger Tolchard (1965-83) 903 (794 ct, 109 st)
Most capped England player David Gower (1975-89) – 106 (11 further caps with Hampshire)

LEICESTERSHIRE

Popular with cricketers, the redeveloped Grace Road County Ground boasts a fabulous indoor cricket school and media centre.

MIDDLESEX

Lord's is simply the most prestigious cricketing venue in the world and is often described as "the headquarters of cricket".

LORD'S, ST JOHN'S WOOD, LONDON

Main tel 020 7289 1300
Website www.middlesexccc.com
Capacity 28,000

First County Match Middlesex v MCC (31 May 1815)
First Test Match England v Australia (21 July 1884)
First ODI England v Australia (26 August 1972)
Record crowd 27,835 Australia v Pakistan (World Cup Final, 20 June 1999)
Formed in 1864
County Champions 1903, 1920, 1921, 1947, 1949 (shared), 1976, 1977 (shared), 1980, 1982, 1985, 1990, 1993
Gillette/NatWest/C&G/FP 1977, 1980, 1984, 1988

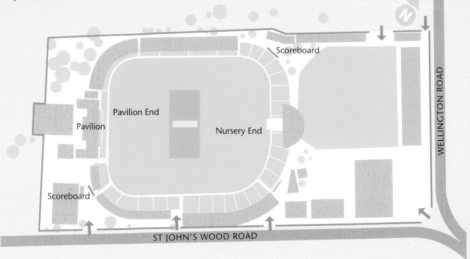

With the glamorous Lord's as its home ground, Middlesex has always been a prestigious county. Its success in the County Championship dates back to the early twentieth century. The club first won the title in 1903 and, while consistent success was hampered by a high number of amateur players, it won the Championship again in 1920 under the leadership of "Plum" Warner. The strong batting line-up featured Harry Lee, Jack Hearne and "Patsy" Hendren, a much-loved man who ended up with more runs and centuries for Middlesex than anyone else; Hearne, with 123 wickets, and paceman Jack Durston provided the backbone for the bowling attack, which also featured the leg-spin of the teenage GTS Stevens. That was Warner's last season for Middlesex: he retired, at the age of 46, having been captain since 1908. His replacement as skipper, Frank Mann, led Middlesex to the 1921 Championship crown.

For the remainder of the 1920s and the 1930s, further Championship success eluded Middlesex, then under the captaincy of Mann and Nigel Haig. However, the club's next title-winning season was particularly memorable. In the glorious 1947 season the "Terrible Twins", Denis Compton and Bill Edrich, between them scored a remarkable 7,355 runs and 30 centuries, and took 140 wickets. With the openers Robertson and Brown both passing 2,000 runs, Middlesex marched towards the Championship under the ever-attacking leadership of Walter Robins despite not possessing a particularly strong bowling attack.

Although Middlesex shared the title with Yorkshire in 1949 the county struggled to live up to these heights for most of the following 25 years, despite the contributions of the off-spinning all-rounder Fred Titmus, wicket-keeper John Murray and batsman Peter Parfitt.

The most successful era in the club's history was from 1976 onwards under the leadership of Mike Brearley, captain since 1971. The 1976 team featured the batting of Graham Barlow and a youthful Mike Gatting and the spin bowling of Titmus, in the last full year of his illustrious career, and the young Phil Edmonds. The Championship was won five times in the decade that followed, and the team also picked up several one-day trophies during this time.

Mike Gatting, who took over from Brearley as captain in 1983, continued the run of success. He was helped by a strong pace attack, featuring Wayne Daniel and Norman Cowans and batting based upon the openers Graham Barlow and Wilf Slack, as well as the veteran Clive Radley. Championship titles followed in 1990 and 1993, with the West Indian opener Desmond Haynes and Mark Ramprakash mainstays of the batting. However, since then the club's high standards have dipped, even though it has continued to supply a number of players to the England team and a return to the glory years was hinted at by the Twenty20 victory in 2008.

Lord's was not always located on the present site. It was named after its owner Thomas Lord, a Yorkshire businessman. Originally, from 1787, it was based in the area known as Dorset Square (in London's West End); it then moved to Regent's Canal, near its present location, in 1811 before moving for the last time in 1814. The ground has been privately owned by the Marylebone Cricket Club since 1866, and started playing host to Middlesex in 1877.

The architecture of the ground is a mixture of the traditional and modern. The pavilion was built in the Victorian era, designed by architect Thomas Verity and completed in 1889-90. Directly opposite the pavilion, which contains the famous Long Room, is the Media Centre at the Nursery End, which was opened in 1999. The spectator stands include the Warner Stand (named after "Plum" Warner and opened in 1958), the Compton and Edrich Stands and the Tavern Stand, which dates from 1967. Other recent stands are the Mound Stand (1987) and the main Grandstand (1997).

"Old Father Time", Lord's famous weather-vane, was moved from the old Grand Stand when that stand was demolished to the other end of the ground in 1996. The ground, located in the St John's Wood area of London, hosted the first three World Cup Finals, in 1975, 1979 and 1983, and again in 1999. It plays host to the Twenty20 World Cup Final in 2009 and will again stage the longer-format one-day World Cup Final in 2019.

Lord's first hosted a Test Match against Australia in 1884. Since then it has showcased the greats of the game, witnessing some amazing achievements along the way. In 1899 the all-rounder Albert Trott, playing for the MCC against the touring Australians, hit Monty Noble over the pavilion at Lord's, the only time the landmark has been cleared. Another Australian, Bob Massie, made a remarkable debut at Lord's in 1972, taking match figures of 16-137 against England. The 1990 England-India Test Match featured a number of records, with Graham Gooch scoring 333 and 123, and Kapil Dev hitting four consecutive sixes off Eddie Hemmings to help India avoid the follow-on.

Lord's contains the head office of the English Cricket Board (the ECB) and was, until 2005, also the headquarters of the International Cricket Council.

Benson & Hedges 1983, 1986
Sunday League 1992
Twenty20 2008
Nickname of one-day team Panthers
Leading run-scorer Elias "Patsy" Hendren (1907-37) 40,302 (av 48.81)
Leading wicket-taker Fred Titmus (1949-82) 2,361 (av 21.27)
Most wicket-keeping dismissals John Murray (1952-75) 1,224 (1,024 ct, 200 st)
Most capped England player Mike Gatting (1975-98) – 79 Tests

While Northants have never won the County Championship, they have finished second on four occasions and won a number of one-day titles. The club was officially formed in July 1878 from an embryonic organisation which is believed to date from 1820 (if this is the case, Northants may well be the oldest of all the counties). After some success in Minor Counties cricket, they were admitted to the County Championship in 1905. The club's first match in the Championship was against Hampshire at Southampton in May 1905.

Northants have never managed to win the Championship, but they have finished runners-up four times. The first was in 1912 (when the county finished second to Yorkshire, losing only one of their 18 matches) but unfortunately for the county's supporters, this was not a prelude to a successful era. On the contrary, the inter-War years were notable for a remarkable stretch of 99 matches without winning a single Championship match between May 1935 and May 1939. Between 1919 and 1948, the county failed to finish in the top ten of the table, finishing bottom in 10 of these seasons.

Performances picked up after 1945, especially under the captaincy of Freddie Brown. Another sign of the county's upward fortunes was the selection of Frank Tyson and Keith Andrew for the Ashes-winning MCC tour of Australia in 1954-55. The captaincy passed from Brown to Dennis Brookes, then to Raman Subba Row in 1958. Northants finished runners-up in 1957, 1965 and 1976 and enjoyed success in the one-day competitions, winning knock-out trophies in 1976, 1980 and 1992. Indeed 1976 was probably the county's most successful season ever, as they beat Lancashire in the final of the Gillette Cup and finished runners-up to Middlesex in the Championship.

The county has been served by some top-quality players, including such England stalwarts as the fast bowler Frank Tyson, batsmen Raman Subba Row (who scored the first triple-century for the club) and Allan Lamb, as well as modern-day spin bowler Monty Panesar. The county has also had a number of overseas star players in the past 30 years, notably Bishen Bedi, Kapil Dev, Curtly Ambrose, Anil Kumble and Matthew Hayden.

Northants played at the Racecourse Ground in Northampton before their move to the County Ground in 1886. The land was bought for £2,000 and the move was given long-term financial backing by Alfred Cockerill. After hosting Minor Counties cricket, the ground finally hosted its first first-class match in June 1905, with Leicestershire the opponents. As well as cricket, the County Ground also accommodated a range of sports including cycling, tennis, athletics, bowls and football. It was the home of Northampton Town FC from 1897 until 1994, when they moved to a purpose-built stadium two miles away.

Since 1990 the ground has benefited from a series of improvements. The pavilion was refurbished in 1990-91 and named the Spencer Pavilion, after Earl Spencer (the Spencers are a prominent local family and the current Earl Spencer, brother of the late Princess of Wales, has a cricket pitch on his estate at Althorp). Its seating capacity was increased by an investment of £100,000 in 1996-97. New entrance gates were constructed in 1992-93 and 1997 at the Wantage Road and Abington Avenue ends of the ground. The latter became the main public entrance, and was renamed the Dennis Brookes Gate. In 1997 an indoor cricket centre was built.

The County Ground hosted two matches in the 1999 World Cup and staged the first women's Test Match in England, England v Australia in 1937. It has also been the scene of some spectacular batting performances: in 2001, the home batsman Mike Hussey scored a record 329 not out against Essex.

THE COUNTY GROUND (WANTAGE ROAD) NORTHAMPTON

Main tel 01604 514455
Website www.northantscricket.com
Capacity 3,500
First County Match Northamptonshire v Leicestershire (5 June 1905)
First ODI South Africa v Sri Lanka (19 May 1999)
Record crowd 21,770 Northants v Australians (4 July 1953)
Formed in 1878 (admitted to the Championship in 1905)
County Champions Best – Runners-up 1912, 1957, 1965, 1976
Gillette/NatWest/C&G/FP 1976, 1992
Benson & Hedges 1980
Sunday League Best – Runners up 2006
Twenty20 Best – Semi-finals 2009
Nickname of one-day team Steelbacks
Leading run-scorer Dennis Brookes (1934-59) 28,980 (av 36.13)
Leading wicket-taker Nobby Clark (1922-47) 1,102 (av 21.26)
Most wicket-keeping dismissals Keith Andrew (1953-66) 810 (653 ct, 157 st)
Most capped England player Allan Lamb (1978-95) – 79 Tests

Pavilion
Wantage Road End
Scoreboard
Scoreboard
Abington Avenue End
ABINGTON AVENUE
N

NORTHAMPTONSHIRE

The club's Wantage Road Ground has been graced by many famous overseas players including Kapil Dev, Curtly Ambrose and Matthew Hayden.

NOTTINGHAMSHIRE

The world's third oldest Test arena, Trent Bridge is currently being redeveloped with new stands, floodlights and an electronic scoreboard.

TRENT BRIDGE, NOTTINGHAM

Main tel 0115 982 3000
Website www.trentbridge.co.uk

First County Match
Nottinghamshire
v Sussex (27 July 1840)
First Test Match England
v Australia (1 June 1899)
First ODI England v Pakistan
(31 August 1974)
Capacity 17,000
Record crowd 35,000
Nottinghamshire v Surrey
(15 May 1948)

FOX ROAD

RADCLIFFE ROAD

Scoreboard

Radcliffe
Road End

Pavilion End

Pavilion

HOUND ROAD

BRIDGFORD ROAD

Formed in 1841
County Champions 1907, 1929, 1981, 1987, 2005
Gillette/NatWest/C&G/FP 1987
Benson & Hedges 1989
Sunday League 1991
Twenty20 Best - Semi-finals 2006
Nickname of one-day team Outlaws
Leading run-scorer George Gunn (1902-32) 31,592 (av 35.69)
Leading wicket-taker Thomas Wass (1896-1920) 1,653 (av 20.34)
Most wicket-keeping dismissals Thomas Oates (1897-1925) 957 (733 ct, 224 st)
Most capped England player Derek Randall (1972-1993) – 47 Tests

County cricket in Nottinghamshire has a long history, and Trent Bridge has hosted county cricket since 1840. "Notts" won the Championship four times in the 20th century and again in 2005. The club was formally constituted in 1841. After its foundation Notts became a significant force in the game, first becoming champion county in 1852 (shared with Sussex) and emerging as the best team in the country in the 1860s and 1870s. Deftly led by George Parr and Richard Daft, Notts had by 1890 won the unofficial championship 18 times.

Nottinghamshire entered the official Championship in 1890, and first won the competition outright in 1907. That season, the brothers George and John Gunn were mainstays of the batting, whilst the most penetrative bowlers were the spinners Albert Hallam and Thomas Wass. The idiosyncratic George Gunn continued to appear for Notts until the ripe old age of 53 – playing the last of his 15 Test Matches when he was almost 51 – and remains the only man to exceed 30,000 runs for the county.

Under the leadership of Arthur Carr, Notts were one of the best sides in the Championship, finishing second in 1922, 1923 and 1927 and winning the Championship in 1929. An important element of their success was the opening attack of Harold Larwood and Bill Voce, who went on to spearhead the England bowling in the "Bodyline" series. Larwood, who had already played a part in England's Ashes triumph in 1926, took 100 wickets in county cricket at an average of 17 the following season and was to remain a major weapon in the Notts attack until 1938.

After the Second World War, Joe Hardstaff and Reg Simpson stood out as elegant batsmen, and the latter took over the captaincy in 1951, in what was a difficult period for the county, characterised by inconsistent performances. Spirits were lifted by the signing of the Australian leg-spin bowler Bruce Dooland in 1952, following lamentable performances in the Championships in both 1951 and 1952; in five seasons, Dooland took 808 wickets, but left in 1957 to return to Australia.

While another top overseas player arrived in the form of Garry Sobers in 1968 (who in one match for the county hit six sixes in an over against Glamorgan), further success proved elusive until the 1980s. It was then that top overseas players, such as the South African Clive Rice (who joined in 1975) and the New Zealand all-rounder Richard Hadlee, joined forces with English talent such as Derek Randall and Tim Robinson, to restore glory to the Trent Bridge side. Championships were won in 1981 and

1987, and a further two one-day trophies were secured in this decade.

Despite some up and down performances in recent times, Nottinghamshire won the Championship again in 2005 under the leadership of another overseas player, the experienced New Zealand batsman Stephen Fleming.

The history of Trent Bridge goes back to William Clarke, the main organiser of the embryonic Nottinghamshire team in the 1830s. After he married Mrs Chapman, the landlady at the Trent Bridge Inn in 1837, the team started playing matches on a ground outside the inn. The Trent Bridge ground evolved from this unlikely beginning, Notts playing their first inter-county match against Sussex in 1840. The ground was also used by the local football side Notts County (the oldest Football League club, formed in 1862) until 1910.

The first Test Match played at Trent Bridge took place in 1899 against Australia (it was the second oldest ground in England to hold a Test after Lord's and the third oldest in the world). The ground stayed in the Clarke family's hands until 1919, when the club purchased it (though a 99-year lease had been signed in 1899).

Parts of the ground are very old – the pavilion was originally designed by HM Townsend and built in 1886 – though it was added to over the course of the 20th century. A famous tree stood behind the Parr Stand, until it was blown down by a gale in 1976; the tree was named after the big-striking batsman George Parr, who famously hit it when playing for the county between 1845 and 1870. Harold Larwood and Bill Voce also have a stand named after them.

In 1990 the William Clarke Stand was built, while the Radcliffe Road Stand was completed in 1998 at a cost of £7.2m. A further £1.9m was spent on the Fox Road stand, which opened in 2002; another redevelopment, costing £8.2m, is due for completion in 2010.

Following its first Test in 1899, Trent Bridge has hosted many notable and exciting Test Matches. Superb batting performances include Denis Compton's 278 against Pakistan in 1954, Tom Graveney's 258 against the West Indies in 1958 and Viv Richards' 232 for the West Indies in 1976. In the 1989 Ashes Test, the Australian opening pair Mark Taylor and Geoff Marsh batted brilliantly, reaching 301 without loss at the end of the first day's play and ended up putting on 329 for the first wicket, the record opening stand in Ashes history. Another Australian batsman, Charlie Macartney, scored a triple century against Notts off 221 balls in 205 minutes in 1921 – the second fastest triple hundred ever; his 345 remains the highest score at the ground.

Above: Trent Bridge. This famous Test ground lies close to Meadow Lane and the City Ground, the homes of Nottingham's two premier football clubs, Notts County and Nottingham Forest. The ground takes its name from the nearby main bridge over the river Trent and it hosted its first Test match in 1899.

Somerset was founded in 1875. From 1882-1886 it fell out of the top tier but its strong record in Minor Counties cricket led to a re-entry to the top flight in 1891, the year after the official County Championship was established. In 1892 it finished third in the Championship.

Somerset's performances for most of the 20th century were patchy, though there were some eye-catching feats along the way. For example, in the three seasons between 1900 and 1902 the only two matches that the all-conquering Yorkshire side lost were both to Somerset; despite this, the Taunton-based county finished 11th, 13th and 7th in those seasons. More typical of their form was that they finished bottom of the Championship in four out of seven seasons in the run-up to the First World War.

A key player in this era was Ernie Robson (1895-1923), who took over 1,100 wickets and scored in excess of 12,000 runs. This period saw the emergence of the slow left-arm bowler Jack White, who played between 1909 to 1937 and took 100 or more wickets each season from 1919 to 1932. One of White's protégés, the spin bowler, Horace Hazell, went on to take 957 wickets in 17 war-interrupted seasons from 1929. The 1930s also saw the rise of perhaps the county's leading home-grown batsman, Harold Gimblett, who scored over 21,000 runs for the county, including 49 hundreds, between 1935 and 1954.

In the mid-20th century there were some low points. The county finished bottom of the Championship several times, including in four consecutive seasons from 1952.

It was only when the Yorkshireman Brian Close assembled a team with the world-class talents of Ian Botham and the West Indians Viv Richards and Joel Garner that the county became a serious force. Close joined Somerset in 1971 and had a huge influence until his retirement in 1977, as a batsman, a fearless short-leg fielder and an ever-optimistic captain. Never previously having won a trophy, Somerset clinched two competitions in the space of two days in the 1979 season: the Sunday League and the knock-out competition, then known as the Gillette Cup. The team won three further one-day trophies in the next four seasons.

Somerset played their first home match at the County Ground in 1882 against Hampshire, and later that season the ground played host to the visiting Australians. Prior to that Somerset led a nomadic existence, playing at many grounds, including Fullands School in Taunton.

The County Ground, by the river Tone, was acquired by the county from the Taunton Athletic Company. It hosted its first official Championship match against Lancashire in 1891. Over the intervening years, the ground has seen a number of redevelopments. The greyhound track which encircled it was removed in the 1970s. The pavilion, originally constructed in 1891, was rebuilt and renamed the Colin Atkinson Pavilion in 1990. The County Ground was where Sir Jack Hobbs scored a hundred in each innings for Surrey to equal and surpass WG Grace's then record number of centuries. It has also witnessed some sparkling batting performances from leading modern batsmen: in 1985 Viv Richards scored 322 runs in one day against Warwickshire and in 1988 Graeme Hick scored his memorable 405 not out for Worcestershire. In the international game, the ground hosted matches at the 1983 and 1999 World Cups, and in 2006 became the home of the England women's cricket team.

The County Ground is currently undergoing a £60m redevelopment, with the aim of completion by 2012. The new Members' Stand and West Stand have already been completed, adding 3,000 more seats to the ground. On the eastern side a new Club Hub is being built, incorporating new changing rooms, gym, office space and restaurants.

THE COUNTY GROUND, TAUNTON

Main tel 0845 337 1875
Website www.somersetcountycc.co.uk
Capacity 7,000 (15,000 with temporary seating for ODIs)

First County Match Somerset v Hampshire (8 August 1882)
First ODI England v Sri Lanka (11 June 1983)
Record crowd 8,450 Sri Lanka v India (26 May 1999)
Formed in 1875 (admitted to the Championship in 1891)
County Champions Best – Runners-up 2001
Gillette/NatWest/C&G/FP 1979, 1983, 2001
Benson & Hedges 1981, 1982
Sunday League 1979
Twenty20 2005
Nickname of one-day team Sabres
Leading run-scorer Harold Gimblett (1935-54) 21,142 (av 36.96)
Leading wicket-taker Jack White (1909-37) 2,165 (av 18.03)

Most wicket-keeping dismissals Harold Stephenson (1948-64) 1,007 (698 ct, 309 st)
Most capped England player Sir Ian Botham (1974-86) – 89 Tests (he went on to play a further 10 Tests when playing for Worcestershire and three Tests when playing for Durham)

SOMERSET

The West Country county enjoyed a golden era in the 1970s and 80s when Sir Ian Botham and Sir Viv Richards both played for Somerset.

SURREY

The famous south London ground at The Oval hosted the first FA Cup Final, the first England football international and the first Test Match in England.

THE OVAL

Main tel 08712 461100
Website www.surreycricket.com
Capacity 23,000

First County Match Surrey v Kent (25 June 1846)
First Test Match England v Australia (6 September 1880)
First ODI England v West Indies (7 September 1973)
Record crowd 80,000 (over the course of a 3-day match) Surrey v Yorkshire (26 July 1906)
Formed in 1845

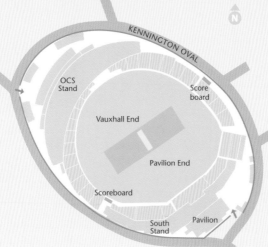

County Champions 1890, 1891, 1892, 1894, 1895, 1899, 1914, 1950 (shared), 1952, 1953, 1954, 1955, 1956, 1957, 1958, 1971, 1999, 2000, 2002
Gillette/NatWest/C&G/FP 1982
Benson & Hedges 1974, 1997, 2001
Sunday League 1996, 2003
Twenty20 2003
Nickname of one-day team Brown Caps
Leading run-scorer Sir Jack Hobbs (1905-34) 43,554 (av 49.72)
Leading wicket-taker Tom Richardson (1892-1904) 1,775 (av 17.87)
Most wicket-keeping dismissals Herbert Strudwick (1902-27) 1,221 (1,035 ct, 186 st)
Most capped England player Alec Stewart (1981-2003) – 133 Tests

The Surrey club was formed in 1845, and has from the outset been based at The Oval. Under the captaincy of Frederick Miller, and boasting leading players such as William Caffyn and Julius Caesar, Surrey was Champion County seven times in the 1850s.

Thirty years later, the second of Surrey's golden ages occurred, inspired by the captaincy of John Shuter and his successor, KJ Key. In 1887, 1888 and (jointly) 1889 it was Champion County. In 1890 Surrey was the first winner of the modern Championship, a crown it was to hold a further five times in the 1890s. The batting was led by the high-scoring Bobby Abel – who made nine double centuries at The Oval, once carrying his bat through the innings for 357 not out, which remains the highest score by a Surrey player – and Tom Hayward, a stylish batsman, the first of five Surrey men to score 100 hundreds and whose 3,246 runs for Surrey in 1906 remain a county record. The key bowlers were George Lohmann and the tireless paceman Tom Richardson.

The successes of the 1890s were not experienced again for 50 years. Surprisingly, in his illustrious 30-year Surrey career the great Sir Jack Hobbs was only once a member of a Championship-winning side, in 1914, although several times his club came very close. Whilst the batting, starting with Hobbs and Andrew Sandham, was very strong, and the respected Herbert Strudwick kept wicket, the bowling was weak. It required all of the ingenuity and boldness of Surrey's canny leg-spinning captain, Percy Fender, to bowl other sides out on the batsman-friendly Oval wickets. Nor did Fender's successor as captain, England's "Bodyline" skipper Douglas Jardine, manage to overcome Surrey's bowling deficiencies, despite the hardworking paceman Alf Gover, who took more than 200 wickets in both 1936 and 1937.

It was Surrey's formidable bowling attack which was the primary reason for their unequalled domination of the Championship in the 1950s. After sharing the spoils in 1950, from 1952 Surrey won seven Championships in a row, the first five under the leadership of Stuart Surridge, the last two under the team's leading bat, Peter May. The bowling was opened by the great Alec Bedser and by Peter Loader, who in 1958 took 9-17 at The Oval against Warwickshire; the spin bowling was in the hands of Jim Laker, whose feat of taking 19 Ashes wickets at Old Trafford in 1956 is unapproached in all first-class cricket, and the combative Tony Lock, with the capable support of Bedser's twin brother Eric. Wonderful support in the field was provided by wicket-keeper Arthur McIntyre and fearless fielders in

the leg-trap, notably Lock and Micky Stewart. In 1956 Surrey won 23 of its 28 Championship matches – and was the first county for 44 years to defeat the Australians.

Between 1959 and 1999 Surrey won the Championship only once, in 1971 under Micky Stewart's captaincy. This was despite the emergence of John Edrich and Ken Barrington as bulwarks of England's batting, and of seamers Geoff Arnold and Robin Jackman – whose 121 wickets in 1980 helped the county to finish runners-up – and off-spinner Pat Pocock; and the fearsome pace of West Indian quicks Sylvester Clarke and Tony Gray.

At the turn of the millennium Surrey once again dominated the county scene, under the inspirational captaincy of Adam Hollioake, aided by coach Keith Medlycott. As well as winning the Championship in 1999, 2000 and 2002, Surrey captured several one-day trophies, with key contributions from Martin Bicknell and Mark Ramprakash. Surrey's aura of success was dented by demotion to the Championship's Division Two in 2005. Whilst promotion as Division Two champions followed the next year, in 2008 Surrey finished bottom of Division One and, for the first time in its proud history, failed to register a single Championship victory.

The story of The Oval dates from 1844 when the Montpelier Cricket Club of Walworth needed a new ground. A lease was obtained on the market garden at Kennington Oval, which was – and remains to this day – owned by the Duchy of Cornwall. Ten thousand pieces of turf from Tooting Common were laid.

The development of the cricket ground helped inspire the formation of Surrey County Cricket Club in 1845. The Oval became its base. In 1880 Surrey secretary CW Alcock arranged for the first Test Match in England to be played at The Oval, when 40,000 spectators watched England, for whom WG Grace scored 152, defeat Australia by five wickets.

The renewal of the lease in 1896 prompted Surrey to build its present pavilion, designed by architect Thomas Muirhead, who had previously designed the Old Trafford pavilion. Over the years The Oval became more dilapidated – during the Second World War it was converted for use as a prisoner-of-war camp but never used for this role. Recently, considerable redevelopment has taken place, including a new north stand at the Vauxhall End and the installation of four 130ft-high permanent floodlights. Financial difficulties have been mitigated by commercial sponsorship deals which have caused the Kennington Oval to be renamed the Fosters Oval, then the AMP Oval and, now, the Brit Oval.

Above: The Oval is often described as a "batting paradise" – more than 135 double centuries have been scored there, including Len Hutton's famous 364 in England's record total of 903 for 7 in the 1938 Ashes Test – but it has also seen famous bowling achievements – including Eric Hollies' bowling Bradman for a duck in his last Test innings in 1948, and Michael Holding's 14 wickets for West Indies in the 1976 Oval Test.

ricket has been played in Sussex for hundreds of years but it is only since the turn of the 21st century that the Hove-based county has won the County Championship, becoming one of the most successful teams of the decade.

Founded in 1839, Sussex is England's oldest county cricket club. Prior to 1855 it won the unofficial championship seven times and shared it once. However, the club had to wait until 2003 to win the official County Championship. After finally breaking its duck, it became the dominant county and won the Championship again in 2006 and 2007 – on the latter occasion only by 4.5 points on the last day of the season after Lancashire failed by just 25 to reach a mammoth 489 to beat Surrey.

Just as the main reason for Sussex's historic failure to win the Championship was their relative weakness in bowling, so it is striking that the most significant contributions to their Championship triumphs were made by the Pakistan leg-spinner Mushtaq Ahmed. The leading Championship wicket-taker for each of the years 2003 to 2007, he took 459 wickets in those five seasons. Most tellingly, he took 83 wickets in Sussex's 10 wins in 2003; 80 in the nine victories in 2006; and 60 in the seven games they won in 2007. Bowling support was provided by James Kirtley; the star batsman was the Zimbabwean Murray Goodwin, who in the Championship-sealing defeat of Leicestershire in 2003 made the then highest-ever score for Sussex, 335 not out – which he surpassed with an unbeaten 344 in 2009.

In the early 20th century, Sussex had an immensely powerful batting line-up, headed by Ranjitsinhji and CB Fry. In 1901 Sussex made six totals of more than 500 and the first-class averages were headed by three Sussex men, all of whom averaged over 70 – Fry (who made 13 hundreds), George Brann and Ranjitsinhji. Ranjitsinhji led the county to second place in the Championship in 1902 and 1903, but the bowling, despite the spin of Fred Tate and George Cox senior, was not quite strong enough for Sussex to finish top.

In the 1920s Sussex were led by Arthur Gilligan. For a short time he and Maurice Tate formed the most devastating bowling attack in the country. Whilst Gilligan's effectiveness was blunted by a blow over the heart when batting, the tireless Tate went on to carry the bowling attack for Sussex, for whom he took more wickets than any other bowler. Tate also scored more than 17,000 runs for Sussex alone.

Sussex enjoyed a golden period in the early 1930s, finishing second in the Championship in 1932, 1933 and 1934. Their nucleus consisted of members of cricketing families who have served Sussex remarkably well over the years: the batting of Duleepsinhji (Ranjitsinhji's nephew), John Langridge, Harry Parks and George Cox junior and the all-round contributions of James Langridge (John's brother) and Harry Parks' brother Jim, who in 1937 performed a unique double by scoring 3,003 runs and taking 101 wickets.

After a poor start following the Second World War, in 1953 David Sheppard led Sussex to second place again. Unfortunately neither he nor Hubert Doggart (who captained the side in 1954) was able to play for Sussex for more than one full season. Between 1960 and 1965 Sussex were captained by Ted Dexter, who led them to Gillette Cup triumphs in the first two years of that competition; Sussex were losing finalists in three of the next 10 years. As well as the powerful hitting of Dexter and wicket-keeper Jim Parks junior, important contributions were made by all-rounder Alan Oakman, paceman John Snow and medium- pacer Ian Thomson.

Under the astute captaincy of John Barclay, in 1981 Sussex, agonisingly, were pipped to second place in the Championship by just two points, but they went on to win the Sunday League the following year and the NatWest Trophy in 1986. However, despite the all-round skills of Imran Khan and the batting of Alan Wells, the county had to wait two further decades before Chris Adams led them to three Championships – while one day titles were won in the 2006, 2008 and the 2009 seasons.

The County Ground at Eaton Road has been the home of Sussex cricket for almost 140 years. When it was purchased in 1871 it was a barley field, but the turf was removed from the club's previous Royal Brunswick Ground and relaid at Eaton Road, where it has remained ever since.

The County Ground is famous for its sea fret, which helps the bowling. On the other hand, on hot and cloudless days batsmen have caused carnage. Duleepsinhji and Eddie Paynter have both performed the rare feat of scoring more than 300 runs in a day, and Murray Goodwin scored a then club record 335 not out in 2003. In 1984 Viv Richards hit a six over the Arthur Gilligan Stand – the ball carried for 130 yards. However, the most famous innings at Hove was played by Nottinghamshire's Edwin Alletson, who in 1911 despite an injured wrist scored a remarkable 189 in 90 minutes, during which he hit 34 runs off one over and 97 in just five overs. One of Alletson's eight sixes smashed the pavilion clock; another damaged the pavilion bar. He scored 142 of the 152 put on for the last wicket in just 40 minutes. Remarkably, it was the only hundred of his career.

THE COUNTY GROUND, HOVE

Main tel 01273 827100
Website www.sussexcricket.co.uk
Capacity 7,000 for Twenty20 (otherwise 4,000)

First County Match Sussex v Gloucestershire (6 June 1872)
First ODI India v South Africa (15 May 1999)
Record crowd 7,800 India v South Africa (15 May 1999)
Formed in 1839
County Champions 2003, 2006, 2007

SUSSEX

The first decade of the 21st century has been particularly successful for Sussex, whose beautiful county ground at Hove lies close to the sea.

Scoreboard

Cromwell Road End

Sea End

Members' Pavilion

Scoreboard

Gillette/NatWest/C&G/FP 1963, 1964, 1978, 1986, 2006
Benson & Hedges Best – Semi-finals 1982, 1999
Sunday League 1982, 2008, 2009
Twenty20 2009
Nickname of one-day team Sharks
Leading run-scorer John Langridge (1928-55) 34,150 (av 37.69)
Leading wicket-taker Maurice Tate (1912-37) 2,211 (av 17.41)
Most wicket-keeping dismissals Harry Butt (1890-1912) 1,176 (911 ct, 265 st)
Most capped England player Ted Dexter (1957-68) – 62 Tests

WARWICKSHIRE

Renowned for having a great atmosphere for international cricket, Edgbaston was the scene of Brian Lara's record-breaking county innings.

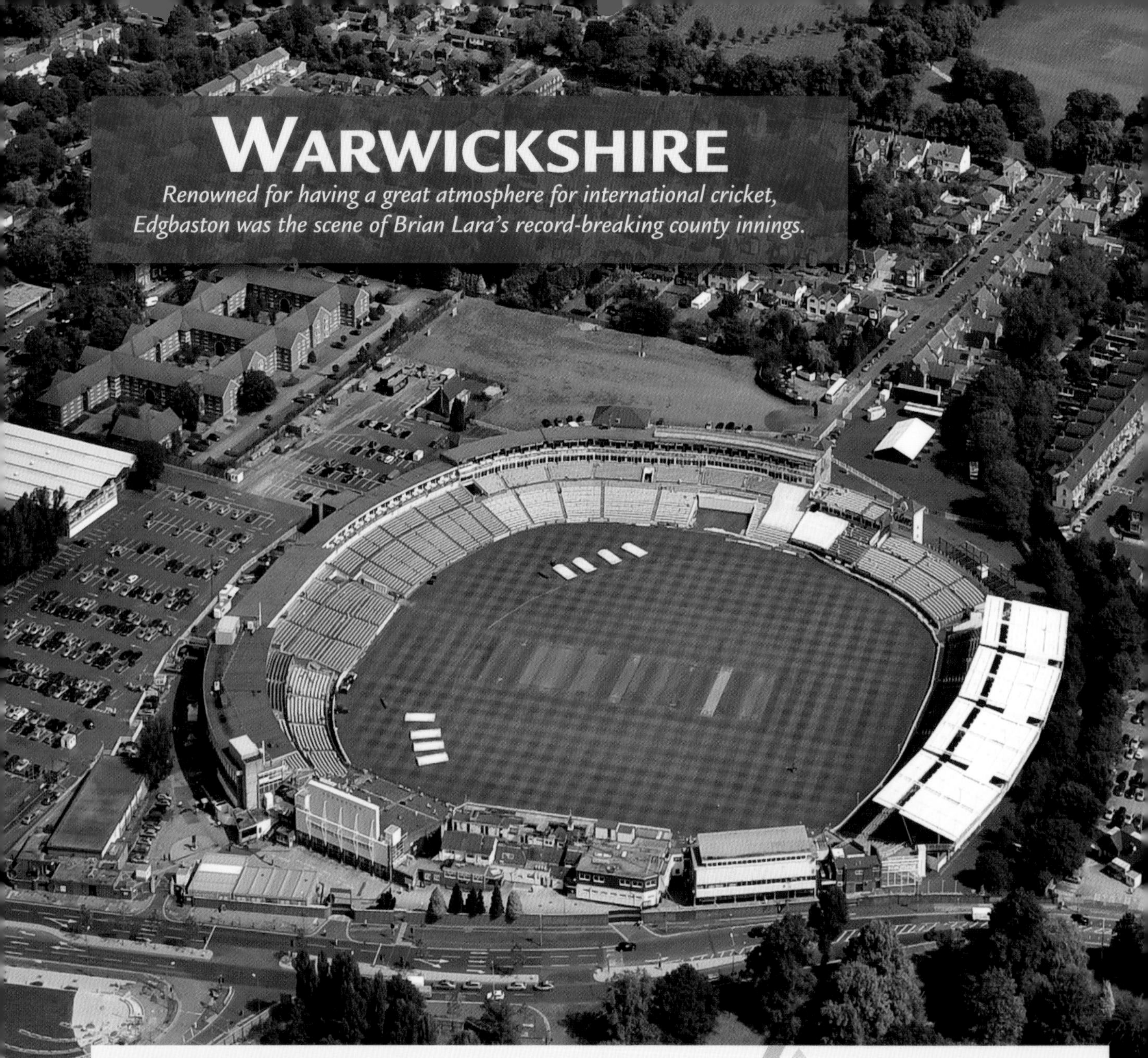

EDGBASTON, BIRMINGHAM

Main tel 0870 062 1902
Website www.edgbaston.com
Capacity 21,000

First County Match Warwickshire v Kent
(14 May 1894)
First Test Match England
v Australia (29 May 1902)
First ODI England v
Australia (28 August 1972)
Record crowd 32,000
England v West Indies
(30 May 1957)
Formed in 1882 (admitted to the
Championship in 1895)
County Champions 1911, 1951,
1972, 1994, 1995, 2004

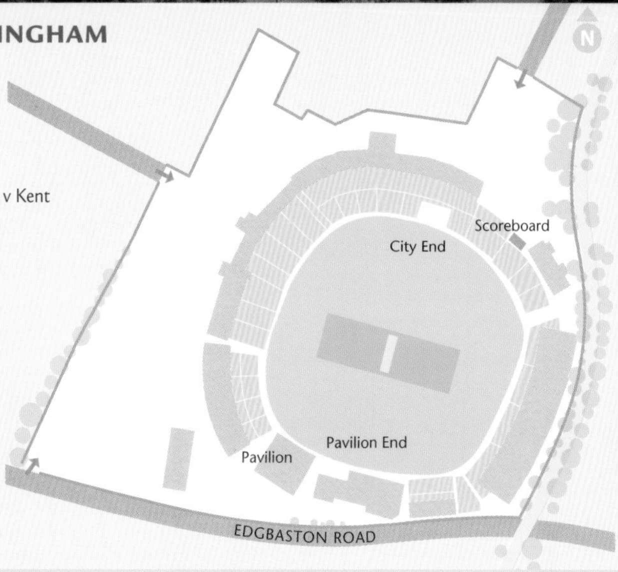

[Stadium plan with labels: City End, Scoreboard, Pavilion End, Pavilion, EDGBASTON ROAD, N]

Gillette/NatWest/C&G/FP 1966,
1968, 1989, 1993, 1995
Benson & Hedges 1994, 2002
Sunday League 1980, 1994, 1997
Twenty20 Best – Runners-up 2003
Nickname of one-day team Bears
Leading run-scorer Dennis Amiss
(1960-87) 35,146 (av 41.64)
Leading wicket-taker Eric Hollies
(1932-57) 2,201 (av 20.45)
Most wicket-keeping dismissals EJ
"Tiger" Smith (1904-30) 800 (662 ct,
138 st)
Most capped England player Bob
Willis (1972-84) -85 (5 caps when
previously with Surrey)

Warwickshire CCC was founded in 1882. Its early results as a county were moderate but in 1911 the county just pipped Kent to the Championship crown. Frank Foster not only proved an inspiring leader in his first year as captain, but contributed mightily with both bat (1,383 runs) and ball (116 wickets with his fast left-arm bowling). Other notable batting contributions were made by Willie Quaife, halfway through a long and illustrious county career, Septimus Kinneir and Crowther Charlesworth, all of whom passed 1,000 runs. Chief bowling support was provided by paceman Frank Field with 122 Championship wickets.

Problematically, Warwickshire's Championship crowns have not created ongoing momentum. The county slipped to mid-table in the three years leading up to the First World War, despite the fine efforts of Foster. During the 1920s Warwickshire did not enjoy success, the bowling being over-dependent on Harry Howell and the captain, the Hon. Frederick Gough-Calthorpe. Bob Wyatt led the county to fourth place in 1934, with strong bowling contributions from JH Mayer and George Paine, but more fallow years followed – even though in 1946 leg-spinner Eric Hollies took a club-record 180 wickets – until in 1951 Warwickshire's first professional captain, Tom Dollery, led his team to the county's second Championship.

Again, however, Warwickshire dropped off after a year of triumph. Under MJK Smith's captaincy between 1957 and 1967 there was an improvement. The captain's own brilliant batting in 1959, when he scored a club-record 2,417 runs, enabled the county to finish fourth. The carefree batting of Bob Barber and big-hitting Jim Stewart (who in a game against Lancashire at Blackpool in 1959 hit a then-record 17 sixes) was complemented by the disciplined pace bowling of Tom Cartwright, Jack Bannister and David Brown. The Gillette Cup was won in 1966.

Under the former England wicket-keeper Alan Smith, who over time recruited four formidable West Indians – stroke-makers Rohan Kanhai and Alvin Kallicharan, wicket-keeper Deryck Murray and off-spinner Lance Gibbs – Warwickshire won the Gillette Cup again in 1968, and clinched the Championship in 1972. Key contributors that season were the four West Indian stars, Dennis Amiss, MJK Smith and fast bowler Norman McVicker – although the bowling averages were headed by Alan Smith. No further triumphs followed in the remainder of the 1970s. The highlight of Bob Willis' five years as captain between 1980 and 1984 was the Sunday League title in his first year as skipper. A

steady decline followed, until under the guidance of coach Bob Woolmer and captain Dermot Reeve Warwickshire became, in the mid-1990s, the leading county in English cricket. After winning the NatWest Trophy in 1993, the following season Warwickshire enjoyed an *annus mirabilis*: it became the first county to win three of the four domestic trophies in a single season and was the losing finalist in the fourth, the NatWest Trophy. While this was very much a team effort, the remarkable contribution of Brian Lara cannot be ignored: he scored 2,066 runs and averaged almost 90.

Warwickshire retained the Championship in 1995, and won the C&G Trophy (the successor to the NatWest Trophy). Demotion from Division One of the Championship was swiftly followed by promotion back to the top flight – and a sixth Championship in 2004 under the leadership of Nick Knight. In a strong batting line-up which yielded 19 hundreds and 49 half-centuries, Ian Bell stood out with six centuries.

The history of Edgbaston began in 1884 when Warwickshire took a 21-year lease of "a meadow of rough grazing land of around 12 acres at a fair and reasonable rental, without harrowing conditions" by the banks of the river Rea in the suburbs of Birmingham.

Edgbaston hosted its first Test Match in 1902. Although rain prevented a result, England dismissed Australia for just 36, Wilfred Rhodes taking 7-17. Just three Tests followed, in 1909, 1924 and 1929, until Test cricket returned to Edgbaston in 1957. In 1994 Brian Lara scored his famous 501 not out, contributing the lion's share of a county record total of 810 for 4.

The return of Test cricket in 1957 followed extensive ground improvements, including the installation of the striking Thwaite Memorial Scoreboard. Erected in 1950 and subsequently transplanted to the City End it is named after Dr Harold Thwaite, a generous President of the Club. Energetic club fundraising helped to pay for the "Brumbrella", a huge motorised cover which protects the whole ground from rain. Further developments followed, including the indoor Edgbaston Cricket Centre, an electronic scoreboard and the imposing Eric Hollies Stand, named after Warwickshire's leading wicket-taker.

On Edgbaston's perimeter wall is the Sydney Barnes Wicket Gate: erected in 1973, on the centenary of his birth, it marks the place where the great bowler entered the ground in 1894 to play his first county match – and where his ashes were placed after his death in 1967. In the pavilion is located the Warwickshire County Cricket Club Museum, where many artefacts of county history are to be found.

Above: Birmingham's Edgbaston ground is to be redeveloped at a cost of £32m. Plans include new conference facilities, permanent floodlighting, a hotel, offices and housing. Once the work has been completed, capacity at the ground will rise to 25,000.

Founded in 1865, Worcestershire County Cricket Club joined the County Championship in 1899, after being Minor Counties Champions for each of the first four years of that competition. In the early days the county was so dominated by the Foster family that it became known as "Fostershire". Between 1899 and 1934 seven Foster brothers played for Worcestershire, and three captained the team. In 1899 RE Foster – whose 287 against Australia in 1903-04 remains the highest score by a Test debutant – and WL Foster each made two centuries in the same match for Worcestershire against Hampshire.

In 1907 Worcestershire finished in second place in the Championship. Thereafter, however, the club struggled. In geography and population the smallest of the first-class counties, it was nearly wound up in 1914, was unable to compete in the Championship in 1919 and in 1920 lost three successive county matches by an innings and more than 200 runs. Things only improved slightly in the next two decades despite the batting of Cyril Walters, "Doc" Gibbons and the Nawab of Pataudi senior. The team was also helped by the effective leg-theory bowling of Fred Root. Root took 207 wickets in 1925 and in 1931 (aged 41) returned figures of 9-23 against Lancashire, both of which remain Worcestershire records to the present day.

In the late 1940s Worcestershire developed a formidable bowling attack, with the fast-medium swing of Reg Perks – who took more wickets for Worcestershire than anyone else – and England spinners Dick Howorth and "Roly" Jenkins, which enabled them to finish third in the Championship in 1949, a year in which Jenkins took 183 wickets.

Under the captaincy of Don Kenyon, Worcestershire won the Championship in 1964 and 1965, the year of its centenary. Its batting had been strengthened by the recruitment of Tom Graveney and all-rounder Basil D'Oliveira, while the county's bowling attack – pacemen Flavell and Coldwell and spinners Gifford, Horton and Slade – provided many victims for wicket-keeper Roy Booth.

Heartened by one-day success, Worcestershire won the Championship again in 1974, with the help of the prolific batting of Glenn Turner and the astute captaincy of Norman Gifford. New recruits Ian Botham and Graeme Hick, who was to go on to score a record 106 hundreds for the county, inspired Worcestershire, led by Phil Neale, to two further Championship titles in the late 1980s and considerable one-day success.

Under the captaincy of Vikram Solanki, Worcestershire have again enjoyed one-day success. In 2007 they won the Sunday League, their first trophy for 13 years, but have experienced ups and downs in the Championship: in the last three years they have been promoted to Division One, demoted, and, finally in 2008 – Hick's last season – restored again to the top flight.

Worcestershire have played more than a thousand first-class matches at New Road, their home since 1899. Many consider New Road the most beautiful of all English grounds. It is instantly recognisable by virtue of its being overlooked by the 14th-century tower of Worcester Cathedral, which owned the ground until selling it to the club in 1976.

Three Worcestershire batsmen – Graveney, Turner and Hick – have exceeded 100 hundreds. Fittingly, all three made their 100th hundred at New Road, Turner going on to make a career-best 311 not out. Other batsmen who have enjoyed batting at New Road include the Middlesex opener Jack Robertson, who in 1949 made 331 not out in one day, and Don Bradman. In four innings in four games at Worcester – the curtain-raiser to each of his four tours of England – the Don massacred the Worcester bowling to the tune of 236 (1930), 206 (1934), 258 (1938) and 107 (1948).

Bowlers have also enjoyed success at New Road. Two – Glamorgan's Jack Mercer and Somerset's Jack White – have taken all 10 wickets in an innings there. Between 1983 and 1999 New Road hosted three one-day internationals. It has not held any internationals in recent years, despite its picturesque setting, at least in part because of its relatively limited crowd capacity.

In each of the 2007 and 2008 seasons New Road's proximity to the rivers Teme and Severn caused it to suffer severe flooding. As a result, New Road was seriously damaged, and games were transferred to Kidderminster. Resisting calls for the club to move permanently from New Road, Worcestershire's chief executive, Mark Newton, pointed out, prosaically, that they could not move as "the ground is not worth anything".

Indeed, Worcestershire have underlined their commitment to New Road by embarking on a major redevelopment. The Members' Pavilion, which has been virtually unchanged since 1899, is to be replaced by the new Graeme Hick Pavilion. The old pavilion is to be taken down brick-by-brick and rebuilt on the site of the Ladies' Pavilion, which is to be demolished. The new pavilion is to be built above the 1 in 150 year flood level, and will feature the Tom Graveney Lounge.

Above: New Road has a beautiful riverside location. But in recent years the grounds have been prone to flooding, especially during the off season. In June 2007 the county's Twenty20 match against Warwickshire was cancelled when the river Severn burst its banks.

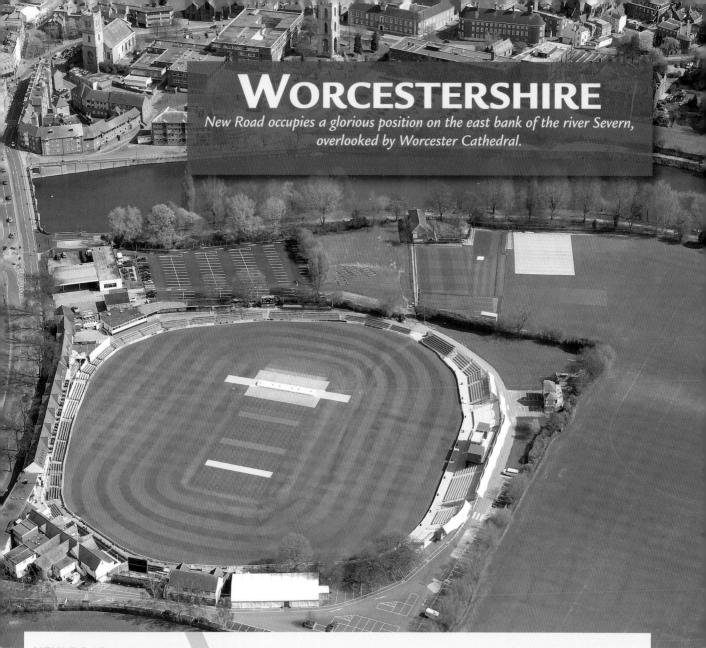

WORCESTERSHIRE

New Road occupies a glorious position on the east bank of the river Severn, overlooked by Worcester Cathedral.

NEW ROAD, WORCESTER

Main tel 01905 748 474
Website www.wccc.co.uk
Capacity 4,900

Formed in 1865 (admitted to the County Championship in 1899)
County Champions 1964, 1965, 1974, 1988, 1989
Gillette/NatWest/C&G/FP 1994
Benson & Hedges 1991
Sunday League 1971, 1987, 1988, 2007
Twenty20 Best – Quarter-finals 2004, 2007
Nickname of one-day team Royals

Leading run-scorer Don Kenyon (1946-67) 34,490 (av 34.18)
Leading wicket-taker Reg Perks (1930-55) 2,143 (av 23.73)
Most wicket-keeping dismissals Steve Rhodes (1985-2004) 1,095 (991 ct, 104 st)
Most capped England player Graeme Hick (1984-2008) – 65 Tests
First County Match Worcestershire v Yorkshire (4 May 1899)
First ODI West Indies v Zimbabwe (13 June 1983)
Record crowd 32,000 (over 3 days), Worcestershire v the Australians (28–30 April 1948)

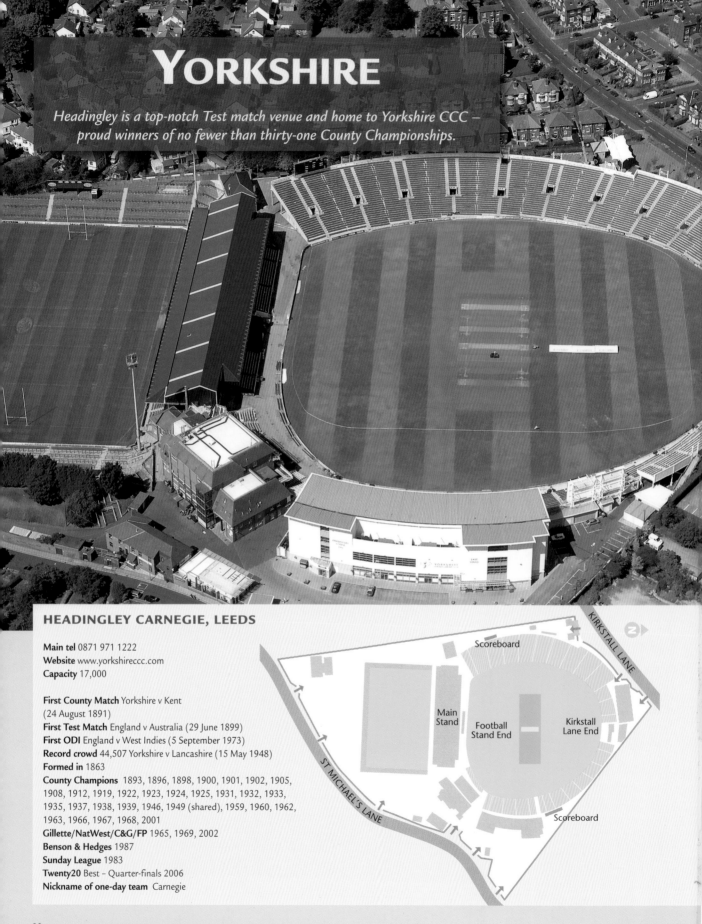

YORKSHIRE

Headingley is a top-notch Test match venue and home to Yorkshire CCC – proud winners of no fewer than thirty-one County Championships.

HEADINGLEY CARNEGIE, LEEDS

Main tel 0871 971 1222
Website www.yorkshireccc.com
Capacity 17,000

First County Match Yorkshire v Kent
(24 August 1891)
First Test Match England v Australia (29 June 1899)
First ODI England v West Indies (5 September 1973)
Record crowd 44,507 Yorkshire v Lancashire (15 May 1948)
Formed in 1863
County Champions 1893, 1896, 1898, 1900, 1901, 1902, 1905, 1908, 1912, 1919, 1922, 1923, 1924, 1925, 1931, 1932, 1933, 1935, 1937, 1938, 1939, 1946, 1949 (shared), 1959, 1960, 1962, 1963, 1966, 1967, 1968, 2001
Gillette/NatWest/C&G/FP 1965, 1969, 2002
Benson & Hedges 1987
Sunday League 1983
Twenty20 Best – Quarter-finals 2006
Nickname of one-day team Carnegie